PLUMS
on the
WALL

KEITH DITTRICH

Lightness fills the air
where heaviness makes
one fight for breath

But you cannot understand this just yet
And there is no way that I can explain it to you
I pray that someday you will, for your sake
But then, alas, you will feel so foolish

Contents

Introduction xiii

A Little Boy's Shadow 1
Bangkok on a Sunday 2
Mental Space 3
Shadows 4
Poem 5
The Six-Thousand-Dollar Sandwich 8
Suds 9
Where It Starts 10
The Splendor of the Day 12
Planets and Friends 13
Your Poetry 14
Moon's Summer Night 15
Untitled 17
You 18
Out of the Canyon 20
Crash Dummies 21
So It Goes 24
Celestial Connection 25
Unfinished Business 26
Of My Nakedness 27
Assessment 30
The Summer of My Life 32
Plums on the Wall 34
Man's Tragic Flaw 35
On Election 37
Light as Feathers 39
Continuum 41

Introduction

It is not by accident that words come together and form thoughts. How does one explain accidental meetings and the coming together of people? Introductions are made and relationships develop. Beyond this, they too are not simply happenstance.

Dreams in our minds, though, seem to be incidental, more random, disorganized, and even beyond. Yet they are outcomes of real experiences, all blended.

Thank you for taking the time to read this little book, which rests between your thoughts and mine. They say visions are where all good things begin. So let us go there.

How did you run into this writing? Was it by accident, or was it not?

It was mine. Now it is yours.

A Little Boy's Shadow

When at night, late evenings,
Laid there, wondering where, why.

There was a dark, shadowy dream that rose as I fell
In fitful sleep after a long day on the farm.

The dark webs of the charcoal-colored dream fixed
With blocks and sticks, the same dark color all mixed—
It moved, and it churned, scared, and it burned.
Times were not good, though grew all the same.

It came again and again,

Waiting by the fence, dry summer wind in my face.

As I grow to my sixties, I remember those nights—
Praying like hell,
Hail Marys time after time.

It must have worked, since I'll call tomorrow,
Though I haven't forgotten and only for sorrow.

I saw you just lately
With the same on your mind.

Bangkok on a Sunday

I wish I were a smoker;
Then I'd step outside this hotel
On an early Sunday morning in Bangkok,
Smoke a cigarette.

I'd watch the streaming traffic go by,
Think of the mother in the alley
Picking nits from her daughter's hair,
Look at the smog-filled sky,

Talk to a taxi driver waiting for a ride,
Offer him a light,
Take a deep draw of my own.
Look at the high-rise cranes, still for the day,
Pass the doorman, and walk back in.

Mental Space

May your dreams lead you to chasms never explored with
Incredible reaches of mental space beyond your
Wildest hopeful possibilities, where
Deep dark explodes into light, promulgating experiences by inexplicable
Interior definitions which engineer places, rooms with
Greatest of social possibilities garnering
Magnetic draws of life, love, prospering experiences that
Grow beyond self to the next into limitless expanses forever,
Beautiful, graceful, soft, boldly promising for all who
Dare to reach epitomes of living, timeless existence spreading,
Blanketing, permeating within an ever-more expanding,
Multidimensional realm!

Shadows

She walks with you, precise steps of your command,
Knowing her place, her duty of keeping the grace,
Goodwill in each step.
A direct connection, she moves with you—
But then, why not, coming from same earth?
We all move in unison; little do we realize,
Though stray for a bit, a lengthening of lines,
Pulled back again by the rules,
Never to run away without you,
Which keeps us in line as we travel through time.
Never wavering much, she flows into space.
There is a fear, though, that pulls her from it—
That haunting pressure she cannot forget.
Run away, run away! From it—get it done.
No more of this; leave me in peace—
Shadow so tall, so perfect in place.

Poem

Maybe
It was the food always on the table,
Or the green sprigs of spring.
How about the autumn-colored,
Tree-lined city streets, bustling
Each morning on his walk
To work, blue sky?

Most stood after the windstorm.

Maybe it was one rainy night
At city square, umbrellas marching,
Or the laugher, the other side of the glass
Panes with evening sconces glowing over white linens.

Could it have been the man huddled
On the concrete stoop at the doorway
With his change can, waiting?

Was it the gray-striped cat peering
From the bushes under the window
As he walked on the cracked sidewalk,
Only partially black?

How about the sound of the subway train
Making it to the stop on Longwood,
Then leaving before he got there?

Maybe it was stone-brown hospital
Buildings in the background
He knew housed sicker people—
Though none sicker in heart—
As he crossed the river way.

Maybe it was the kind innkeeper
Who pointed to all these things
As he walked out the kitchen door
Each morning
With her sternly saying,
"No!"
Believing in him.

Could it have been the bloodstains
On main street by broken glass, tire marks,
Not wanting to leave more dark colors
For someone to try and erase?

Might it have been a poem,
Some written word,
An unspoken thing?
A gesture,
His gesture,
A feeling of disconnected
Connectedness?
Probably it was all of these things.
It was a lovely daughter,
Another lovely lady.

Some hope that there
Had to be something left
From the ruins—
The broken, broken heart
That might be reshaped
Into a new one,
Made from tiny pieces,
Shards,
Green sprigs,
Some blue sky, and
Water.

Remaining love
As the glue to bond it

All together—

Yet,
Maybe, it never quite ends.

The Six-Thousand-Dollar Sandwich

He handed it to me so nonchalantly
As I visited the small bungalow after school,

A grove of trees all around in the windows,
The old kitchen, biggest room in the house,
Pink walls and tired white steel cabinets.

Egg scrambled so easily while we spoke,
Folded in Wonder bread, then given to me.

This kid of fourteen years who just lost his mom,

Hell-bent, singing, screaming in the shed,
Shared with me what he could offer in return.

A home—we wanted to help, so fixed the house roof
So they could live there, broken, drinking dad and all
Crumbling more than the house offered.

We tried hard to make it habitable and happy—
Maybe even a horse in the pasture by the old barn
For those left behind by Mom, shuddering in pain.

I received as he gave; the moment was etched:
The best sandwich I will ever eat.

They left a month later before the state took the kids,

Bulldozed the house next spring, lest I do it again.

8

Suds

At Zio's, we all gathered
To dine and toast well,
Three cultures united
Before the big day,

Then practiced once more
They circled; they spun
He cried out commands;
Hard work, they perfected

The suds ran with sweat
From his back, tired, still strong,
The last wash, another kiss,
Rest, well-earned in his stall.

Soon the dance, the roses,
Accolades and prizes
Worth much more now—
The next day, he must sell.

It's one a.m.; tomorrow here.
Clocks play as we drive;
Ice cream provides the stop,
Just her and I.
Yet,
Time slips away.

Where It Starts

I'm not over you.
A line that offers hope of renewal,
Of only a relationship, a love lost for the moment
That comes back after painful days and sleepless nights.

Though what if there were really more than that—
More than just one, but about the whole?

Dream, my friend, about that.

Dream at night and by day of the whole of us in love again,
In love with each other, all floating in a universal circle, adrift in the
beautiful space we call earth, the abyss—

Each other, animal, fish, plant, creature, tree, and limb,
Each molecule that makes up who we are.

Dream of reverence,
That religion we try to explain through things like God, godlike
things,

Make no exceptions.

Dream of where I want to go.
Most literally, then, follow—
Much larger than one, greater than anything.

The dream takes us to a place that is happy and peaceful, where there is not too much work or strife.
Struggle for this instead.

Your dream will become others' dreams as well.
Pretty soon, you are a dream yourself,
A placemark in the minds of others:

Most beautiful, most reassuring, most spectacular.

The Splendor of the Day

If I might just have
The pleasure of your company—

A sugar-filled talk,
Cinnamon toast for you,

Sweet lines,

Blueberries, apricots,
Peaches and cream for me.

Aromas blend with the
Sound of our words.

No airs in the room—
Just warm breezes.

A prescience of others
Brings forth the day.

Planets and Friends

If planets have friends,
Then the moon must be
Earth's closest.

As friends do,
It bathes its ally in light
At the darkest moments,
Soothing the night
When it can.

Though they can't be there always,
Just knowing, so close
On the other side
Makes all the difference.

Shedding light—
Not just any light,
But a most perfect,
Evening-soft glow,
Never cold
Or hot,
Never sad,

Gray snow blanket
Shimmering on pines,
Frosted grass
Cast in pale light.

Your Poetry

Whispers in my ear,
Soft, lovely thoughts,

Mind now soothed,
Murmurs only expressed—
Vanquish; then vanish.

Falling into sleepy dreams,
Offering deep, quiet moments—
Mysteries, most interior mind,

Residues left of wonderment—
Who am I, really?
What is all this outwardly?

Where must I find myself,
Lost in the inward,
Endless expanse, reaching?

New spaces beget only
More expanse,
Searching till the end.

Moon's Summer Night

Rising downstream,
Across the river it follows—
A turn, dark, shimmering line.

Murmuring a soft utter on the
Waters,
The cows low;
Calves return back.
Coyote calls;
In the distance,

Crickets.

Moving stream,
Stillness of night—
My lights go out on the
Bridge.
Quiet village lights ahead,
Meadows grove,

Moon rises.
Should I race to the next,
Catch it again?

Or let it pass over?

I drive into town,
Just south a little,
And there it is again!
Moving with me,
Following

My dreams of some
Connection
Over the steeple,
The water tower
Large, luminous.

I drive home.
It greets me again.
Fall in bed,
The glow
In my window
Till my eyes close,
Now captured
On the other side.

It dances
In my dreams
With fancy ladies—
My fancies,
Love's softness
Touching,

Moonlight's
Blue haze.

Untitled

London
Bridges come falling down.
Golden hair over shoulders,
Her glasses drop too.
Eyes meet—
Softness between us
As I fall for you

You

Beautiful love, the music is words.
My piano letters key expression;
The song is "You."
Playing again,
Heart pounds out a beat
All for you, my love.
Beautiful love, my music is word.
These lines from beneath,
Soft melodies and rhyme,
Our rhythm complex.

*****

Deep, dear love, dark pools,
Waters swirl
Faster, then faster,
Pulling us down farther
And farther.
We succumb to the depths,
Dark fluidity encompassing
Bodies' arms outreached
Upward,
Hands, fingers softy pointed
Toward the surface far above now.
Legs, feet reaching down, toes—
No bottom; we fall through
The murky abyss.

Vibrations, reverberations,
Colder and colder—
Ice form crackles, shimmers.
Mirror we see in ourselves,
Sunlight flickers above,
Naked bodies in a sky of water.
Water becomes air,
Breathes of fluidity,
In and out.
Pink seahorses gallop
Aside where we swim, swirl.
Our hair floats like seaweed,
Drifting in currents.
We turn, embrace, kiss,
Kissing human fish.
My mermaid of the sea,
Forever pulled down,
Her lovely domain
Beyond human.

Beyond humans forever—
No one will reach us.
Was it the music?

Out of the Canyon

But no!
I believe in redemption—
Or I am no better?.

The miserable few

Who sense is lost for a time
And lead all who might follow

Too many

And what about me,
Lost in the canyon sometimes too
Save me! Save myself
Scour myself with water and sand

May I lead better

Even the miserable few
Or steer the others up the path
To skies of blue
Through lush grasses
Blowing in summer's breeze
Bits of grime whisked away
Till only bare souls

Live on the edge of time

Crash Dummies

A funny thing happened on the dark highway
Last night
As I was traveling to the big city
There on the other side of the median
Someone
Had left a car in the middle of two lanes
Broken,
Destroyed.
Lit a small fire up front near the exposed motor
And left a crash dummy in the driver's seat

Turned around to look at it, I did
Thought it should be put out
But didn't have even a cup of water.

Someone came with an extinguisher,
The dummy was as dummies usually are
Not moving.
The roof was peeled back, so I could see
Its head with broken glass covering over it
The chest was laid back in the seat
Maybe some sensors got hit, went off

By the time an extinguisher got there,
The fire was getting bigger
I stood by,
Aghast,
So I thought I would go find another

Surely they wouldn't want the dummy to
Burn.
Opening the door was futile
Though I tried a little

The dummy kept quiet the whole time.
I drove down the line of cars, waiting
To see if I could find another extinguisher

There was one
So I quickly drove back
The sheriff flew by
Nearly colliding
Just behind him then
At the blazing scene
He said, Get back!

The flames were licking the dummy now
How sad to see it burn.

There I stood froze while he cooked

The glow let me see well.

I wonder how the numbers will turn out
On the crash test in the evening?
Probably not good
Not good, I bet

Crash dummies.

God, help me
God, help him

Why didn't I put my hand on his chest
Hold his hand as he took his last breath

Touch his smashed head that held him?
I did pray for his soul.
Could I have not found a bucket of water?
Or turned his vehicle around to stop
The wind blowing flames to him?
Or pulled the car to the river to water??
These things I didn't do,
Swearing I'd help the next time
Returning the favor of my salvation
From same.

God, help me make my brain work faster

Next time.

Who cares about a crash dummy, though?
They make new ones.
Both of us burned.

So It Goes

As if the rain falls down
To wash away tears
I sleep with it and them

An open window
Or opening window

The sweet sound of drops
On flowing stream water
Upon summer's corn

When darkness falls
They pervade silence
All beautiful, all here

All now

Celestial Connection

Lying there in the night, I think.
Quiet, only the old farmhouse can
A window to the east offers moonlight
From the sun, now cooled, a bluish haze

The quilt angled open, leaves my chest bare
The moon high in the window now
A ray, two rays connected us
My being and the beautiful place above

I only hear my heart beat.

My left arm folded up
The shadowy muscle soft
In submission of my fragility
Amid the magnificence,

Worlds, on both ends of the beam

Unfinished Business

Who goes there now beyond the pale?
Darkness alone holds no light,
I then must find my way
Beyond this space
To light of day

What fear should I have after that night
Death skirted the edge of my face
Left its mark on me
Pain now the driving force
That grips you in fear

Yet,

So little it means, given other affairs
World forces tout crazy leaders
Hell,
Threatens to take it all away
Us with little power

Old men warned
Of our ultimate fate.

Of My Nakedness

If I'd taken my clothes off,
And they saw me naked
It would've been so minor of
An event
If it was just clothes
But it was my soul,
Exposed

You
Accompanied me through
My Hell;
Shared in my happiness,
Joy of living;
Watched me receive
Another chance

Have seen my dark mysteries,
Miseries
Ate of the flesh of my pain
The Benedalor experience
Watched me wallow in sorrow
Of personal losses
Heard me rail on my weakest,
Saddest, shallowest human
Afflictions
Read my deepest words

Who am I?

I have told you
For better or for worse
Naked?
That's nothing
But beauty of the human
Existence
Somehow poised on this earth
For all too see.

Except for the masks
Which hide more than skin
White
Bursting air

Flesh all the same.
Thank the Lord for this body!
Divine, I embrace,
Hold it tightly,
Lay prone with it
Beneath the heavens
My cup runneth over

******

Yet,
Waters lap the dark shore
The landing is soon
I float lifeless, washed
To sands
Of time run out

For who might you be,
Who finds me?
Please carry with kindness
The naked body

This soul-left piece
Absolve me of my sins
Lest I roil forever
Close my eyes
For I drift with the stars now
I am the Grace, the Divine
My children,
My friends,
My animals,
My lovers,
Look for me there.

Please, please
Dance the next dance
In memory of me
Make it a slow one
Hold on tightly,
Closely
Whisper in their ear
Smell of their body,
Feel their soft touch.
Float with the song,
Drift off together,
Away

In the loveliness.

Assessment

Have you ever really assessed yourself,
Taken your spread hands to your chest,
Then moved them down to your stomach

Have you ever studied your own eye
As you would a friend or lover

A hand uncovering your genitalia
Exposes flesh not so beautiful,
Though it began your
Beautiful children

Legs, then knees, your hands work down
Smooth with bumps at the joints
Which move fluidly year after year

For you

Your feet, a bony series of lines
Toes, nails, and padding
Have carried you for years;
They continue to do so

Lying here, all systems are working
Your heart is beating, blood flowing

When touching your face, only fingertips,
Since somehow tenderness must surface

Here, exposed, amusing given the old lines
Creases, weathering, weathered mind
Some hair still shields the skull
Which holds something I can't touch
Nor explain, though it forms these words
In it, contains your life's thoughts,
Life's efforts, struggles, happiness, joy,
All your love,
All your dreams.

The Summer of My Life

Quietness continued
Long after the moments
Of dark entrapment

This morning yet
I sit with nature
Though
Bright streaming sun

Over the banked clouds

A few remaining raindrops
Of last night's shower

Or was it just rain

A year passes
So fine
Changing seasons
Recovering
Now again summer

Death is so close
Or was
Darkness turned green

Nature had called me
Back
To make dust for
Some other existence

Yet here I am
Quiet all along
Lying in the bed

Driving again down
Roads
Inside my mind
Mostly beautiful
Sometimes

Screaming

Plums on the Wall

May they rot in hell on their journey
A slithering fate whose mother of all
Prepared them for such glorious ends

Plums on the wall purple and blue
Pasted there years ago, though
Until this moment couldn't tell you
Much more than colors or hue

Decidedly so, they hunt for us now,
Uttering ghastly images beneath
Never seen till drunken complete

We wallow; our walls are there
Fenced in blindness,
Bar any return

Damn them, damn the damned.
Doomed are we all

Man's Tragic Flaw

We walked hand in hand through the rubble,
Stepping over pieces of bodies.
Some were our friends.

Others, those who helped cause complete devastation,
Now reduced to the same.
Dust settled on us.

Gray soot masking the faces strewn about.
The mix of pain and love between us,
Our hands held tight,

Coursing, confusing, confounding.

What was left in this demise of human existence?
All pain was gone save for what's inside ourselves,
All that was

Us.

Now, the only living example:
Universal love remaining.

Like horses on an arid landscape,
We walked,
Then we ran

Until breathless.
Then we stopped.

Nothing had changed.

Our duty to begin the process,
Populating the earth through our love.
Clasped hands,
Embraced lying.
We held a precious existence.

Nothing would stop us.
Our species needed another chance—
Hope on our galactic deserted island.

Yet knew that in this,
In each of us,
The trace ingredient that caused it again.
Since it always has been
A Sapiens-made flaw.

Night would soon come.

On Election

The winter winds have come howling down from the north,
Though so pleasant not too many days ago.

We reach for hope that all is not lost.

There, so close by, it hangs on a stem.
Leaves green and shiny, a holdout from summer days.

The tea rose had been transplanted once,
Then grew well in fertile soil.
Maybe it will grow again, though a
Terrible and long drought is coming.

I have withstood smaller droughts before.
In my youth, a dry, dusty, starkness.

The fragrance will not be the same, if at all.
Barren stems, blighted leaves, withering blooms.

More painful now, watching others strain, knowing that this rose
may not bloom ever as beautiful again,
If at all.
Hope sleeps in the pod that will ultimately fall to the ground and lie
dormant

Until the conditions are right for it to sprout and grow anew.

If the winter winds do not stop or the summer drought does not end,
There still must be something that survives and springs to life, simply
unbeknownst to us now.

Out of darkness, somehow, there comes a light.

Light as Feathers

The pillow chosen
To rest a weary head
Makes the difference.

A proper fill level—
Down is best choice—
Which cradles the neck
That carries your blood.

If it fits right,
An immediate pleasure
Arrives, then ensues.

Its neighbor is needed
To block remnants of light
From waning sky,
Masking shadows
Or delaying the inevitable
Surfacing of day.

Returning realities
Covered by night.

Choose well
Where laying your head,
Or the pillow itself
May provide the ache
You so had hoped
To vanquish.

The ache has no mercy,
Swallowing the body,
Trying the brain.
The only release then
Comes by light of day.

Continuum

The Parker house—
No ghosts, no shadows
Tucked in quiet corners,
Still missing the spirits
Of a famous old inn
Everything in the room
Must be rediscovered
Unbroken glass, tattered carpet,
Repainted walls,
Windows.
Door to the hallway, more doors,
Mysteries.
Memories surfacing, fading,
Sparkling stars, indigo expanse,
Flashes
In my room.
Angels dance
Over ghosts of past.
Pleasantries: How are you?
I am fine
In these unexplored corners.

A reminder of
Summers gone by
And days to come

www.ingramcontent.com/pod-product-compliance
Lightning Source LLC
Chambersburg PA
CBHW031615040426

42452CB00006B/528